THY WILL BE DONE
Three Principles for Godly Living

by

Nicholas Fuerst

RoseDog Books
PITTSBURGH, PENNSYLVANIA 15238

RoseDog Books
585 Alpha Drive
Suite 103
Pittsburgh, PA 15238
Visit our website at *www.rosedogbookstore.com*

ISBN: 978-1-4809-6841-7
eISBN: 978-1-4809-6818-9

To my wife Patricia,
and my sons Kris, Matthew, and Michael
who inspired the prayer and thinking
which culminated in these concepts.

Acknowledgments

Reverend Michael Conway, Immaculate Conception Parish, Washington, PA – theological proofreading and advisement.

Kaitlin McCracken – my friend, transcriptionist, and literary advisor.

Patty Fuerst – my wife and best friend forever – without whom I would not be who I am.

CONTENTS

INTRODUCTION

When I was a young man and just married, I found myself with my wife, Patty, raising one, then two, and then three sons – Kris, Matthew, and Michael. I often pondered exactly how I could transmit to them an awareness of God's existence and omnipotence; and beyond that, an awareness of their need to recognize and carry out the work that God had planned for them in this life time. By that point in life, my own religious experiences and faith commitment had made me fairly confident that my faith in God was likely going to be sufficient to lead me safely through this life, and on into the promised immortal and eternal life in His presence. But how could I transmit my precious faith in God to my sons, so that they too could achieve that ultimate goal? I had a very strong sense that if in my quest to achieve eternal peace and happiness for myself, I had never bothered to transmit the necessary saving faith to my own God-given children, then maybe this failure, in and of itself, would be sufficient grounds for the Almighty to actually exclude me from it also.

I knew well that a Christian father was expected to lead his family, and to be the head of the spiritual household. I felt a sense of loneliness in this responsibility. If I didn't do it, then it wouldn't get done. There was no other father in the household. Viewing my role in this way, I sensed that it was me, and only me, to whom God had given these three children to father, to shepherd, to teach, and to guide. What a daunting task and heavy burden. But God was the one who bestowed it on me. He must have felt in His plans that I was capable of doing it for His honor and glory. What an awesome gift that my God, the God of history and the God of the Universe, had bestowed on me to father these three boys.

As with most parents, I presume all parents, I had never been formally instructed in the "A-B-Cs" of parenthood. So where was I to start? What was I to do? Of course I had plenty of opportunities to learn by how I observed other parents functioning in childrearing. Mainly, of course, my own parents, but also parents of my friends and relatives. Early in my life I had developed a deep and sincere sense of honor and respect for grown-ups, and so I felt that parents always knew what they were doing in raising their children. As it turns out, they were just basing their actions and parenting styles on things they themselves had observed in times past; things that in obvious or subtle ways had been passed on to them; things that they had construed for whatever reason to be the right ways of doing it. I myself came eventually to appreciate that some of the ways that I was parented and that my friends were parented were right and good, and some were not. Reflections on such experiences allowed me as a young parent to realize that in this crucial responsibility of raising my own children, I had both the freedom and the obligation to figure out ways to do it "right." And so it was my job, my calling, and my mission to filter out the un-Godly and choose the Godly ways to raise my sons.

As time went on in the young lives of my children, my focused attention to this issue of Godly parenting and childrearing convinced me of three specific principles that I was eventually able to articulate. The first one I identified as, "Hold on to your faith."

For those who have been gifted with faith in God and its promise of eternal life and happiness, there is nothing in this world that could possibly be more precious. The second principle was the frequently used admonition spoken by Jesus so many times in the Christian Scriptures, "Be not afraid." With the Good News that is Jesus Christ, there is truly nothing in this world for a person of faith to fear. And the third principle that I came to define was a natural extension of having faith in God, and being courageous in going forth in one's life, "Serve well!" People of Godly faith and purposes need to serve their fellow man with Godly intent; to serve others as exemplified by Jesus' service to mankind; to serve others, as much as possible, with a joyous attitude and a loving heart.

Throughout my parenting years, I referred often to these three principles as I accompanied my sons through the good times and bad times of their growing up processes. This approach to parenting definitely gave me a sense of being organized in transmitting and encouraging Godly and Christian awareness in my sons. I had heard a saying that "Religion is not so much taught, as it is *caught!*" There may be truth to this cliché, but I was not so naive as to "swallow" it and allow myself to think that I could get lazy and somehow justify to myself that I could minimize or abandon the intentional spiritual and religious instruction of my children. But it certainly emphasized to me that I would have to "put my money where my mouth was" and "practice what I preached." So, yes, it was going to be important for me to teach the Catholic faith to whatever degree I could by the conversations I had with them, and the things I said. But also, I needed to demonstrate the faith to them by the things I did in my own spiritual and religious life, as well as in my own personal, professional, and married life. Things they could observe and think about, and at some point decide for themselves if perhaps those things were part of the "right" way to live for themselves.

Did they want to be centered on and to focus on similar ideals as "dear old Dad," or did that not make sense to them at all?

Patty and I stand later in life now having completed our parenting and child raising times. As I look back in judgement of my own efforts to transmit the Christian faith to my sons, so that they might eventually themselves achieve Godliness both in this life and on into eternity, was I a good and Godly parent in how I raised my kids? I don't know. But I do believe that I made a sincere effort to do so. Could I have done better? Absolutely! Was it good enough to secure my eventual eternal reward, and the possibility of theirs as well? Someday, I know, in the presence of God Himself, I will get the answer to that question. In the meantime, I am continuing to focus on these three principles in living out my own Christ-centered life. I have also used them in reinforcing and supporting others who are trying to follow Christ. And now I am publishing them for you to read about and consider as an approach to your own life, whether you are actively parenting children or not, in identifying and carrying out a holy and Christ-centered life. May God's blessings come upon you as you read the following pages.

· · ·

After each chapter's description of its respective principle, I have included in print the words of a particular Christian hymn that I feel reflects that same principle. Although obviously, I cannot include the music that goes with the words, some readers may recall the melodies. I myself, and I believe most people, find music to be something that usually "speaks" to my deepest inner being and inspires me. So I offer these hymns with each chapter's contents as something the reader may reflect on and associate with the principle being discussed.

CHAPTER I:

HOLD ON TO YOUR FAITH

Starting Out

I'm what's sometimes referred to as a "cradle Catholic." I was born the third of six children to Catholic parents who themselves had been born and raised as Roman Catholics. As part of their Catholic duty, they practiced their beliefs "by the books" and with discipline. They consciously shared their faith with us by their words and actions. Not that they were perfect parents or perfect Christians – none of us are. But Mom and Dad were certainly willing Christians who consciously lived their Christ centeredness.

Like my sisters and brothers, I was baptized as an infant, way before (obviously) I could have any understanding or memory of it. I clearly recall at a very early age, possibly as young as four or five, having a deep sense in my heart of feeling "good" about Jesus. I felt a warmth, a connection, and a friendship with Jesus. I felt loved and protected by Jesus. It wasn't really until much later in life, way beyond childhood, adolescence, and early adulthood, and certainly way beyond receiving the sacraments of Reconciliation,

Holy Communion, Confirmation, and even Matrimony, that I came to a much fuller and more complete understanding of what that baptismal event really was. Up until that point, I certainly had an awareness that I had indeed been baptized. The authentic looking Baptismal Certificate, a faded black and white photograph, and my parents' assurances, all convinced me of that. So I was certainly able to accept the fact that Original Sin had been removed from my soul, and that I had been initiated into the Christian faith and the Catholic Church. But what I had not comprehended until later in life was that it was my parents who, by bringing me to the Sacrament of Baptism as an infant, had claimed me for the purposes of Jesus Christ. At that point I wondered when, if ever, had I myself decided that I truly wanted to choose devotion to Jesus Christ to be my way of life? When, if ever, had I claimed myself for Jesus Christ? And I eventually came to the awesome realization that the words and actions of my life up until that time spoke loud and clear that I already had, even early on in my life, accepted my friend Jesus as the center and most important focus in my life. In that sense I had, long ago, claimed myself for Jesus Christ and His purposes both in this world and on into eternity. When I finally recognized this, I was both astounded and ecstatic, and I knew that the ongoing commitment to Jesus in the context of my Christian faith, and the Catholic Church, could secure my joy and fulfilment during the present lifetime, and unending peace and security with God as Father, Son, and Holy Spirit in eternity.

What is Faith?

If we consider a definition for the word "faith" from a dictionary of the English language, we find descriptions of "unquestioning belief that does not require proof or evidence," and "complete trust, confidence, or reliance," and "allegiance to some person or thing; loyalty." If we consider the definition of faith as found in the Catechism of the Catholic Church we find, "Faith is man's response to God who reveals Himself and gives Himself to man, at the same time bringing man a superabundant light as he searches for the ultimate meaning of his life." If we thoughtfully consider each of these descriptions, I think we will have a good basis to discuss faith in God, and the principle of "Hold On To Your Faith."

The content of this book focuses on the Christian religious faith, which is most basically and succinctly stated as the belief in the reality of God as the Father, the Son, and the Holy Spirit – the Holy Trinity. These three Persons clarify all that we are and all that we are meant to be. We can be confident through our faith in them as our God, as to how we and all things have been created; as to the promise of eventual eternal salvation in Heaven; and as to the promise of the love and inspiration that can maintain our focus and our hope as we strive to do the necessary preparation during our lifetimes.

Christianity derives from the story of God's work with Jesus as the Chosen One, the Christ, the Messiah. Jesus, the Son, was divine being truly God, but was also truly human. He lived alongside mankind for a few decades in history. He fulfilled the prophesies of the Hebrew Scriptures, and focused on the reality of the Triune God by his life's work and teachings. Most importantly, His death and Resurrection from the dead, assured all of mankind in all of human history that there was the possibility of eternal life in the eternal Kingdom of God. This is called the "kerygma." It is the story that Christians have claimed to believe in ever since the time of Jesus. "Kerygma" is referred to by Sherry Weddell in her book entitled *Forming Intentional Disciples*. She calls it "the nucleus of the Gospel that awakens Christian faith." She says that this "'Great Story of Jesus' leads a person to be able to say, 'Jesus is Lord!' Kerygma is what Pope John Paul II described as 'the initial ardent proclamation by which a person is one day overwhelmed and brought to the decision to entrust himself to Jesus Christ by faith.'"

In his book *Jesus of the Gospels*, Anthony Zannoni states, "Christian life's essential character is a faith relationship with the person of Jesus Christ. (Faith) is an unmerited gift. (It) is a grace! Ultimately, we can only grasp the mystery of who Jesus is through the eyes of faith."

The mystery that one encounters in the Christian faith was aptly stated by Monsignor Ronald Knox in his book, *A Retreat for Lay People*.

"A commitment to Jesus Christ is not a commitment to understanding, but rather it is a commitment to faith. Jesus does not ask us to understand. He asks us to believe. It is the very nature of faith to thrive on mystery."

How is Faith Acquired?

In considering how it is that one comes to acquire faith in Jesus Christ as the One who reveals the true person and nature of God, I find great excitement in the Gospel story of Jesus meeting the Samaritan woman at Jacob's well. In this story (John 4:5-42), the woman has an apparent chance encounter with Jesus as she comes to the well to draw the water that is necessary to sustain her mortal life for that day. Instead she discovers the source of the living water (Jesus Himself) that will sustain her on into immortality in the eternal life. By listening to the words of Jesus, she becomes convinced of who He truly is – the Anointed and Holy One of God and the Messiah who was so long awaited by the Jewish nation. With the thrill of her newly realized faith, the woman hastens back to town and spreads the good news to others. They in turn go out to the well to experience for themselves the words and the person of Jesus. In doing so, they too came to believe in the real presence of their Savior.

I have to think that this is the way anyone comes to believe in Jesus as the Christ, and as the center of his life. Not a chance encounter but rather, like the woman at Jacob's well, a Providential plan, an unmerited gift, and a grace from God. Such an encounter with Jesus changes a person because he must now decide for himself whether or not he will make the Good News of Jesus Christ the focus of his life. A true and bona fide encounter with Jesus demands a change. One must choose either to believe in Him as the Chosen One of God, or not. One must choose to accept Him as the Lord and Master, the Redeemer and Savior of his life, or not. Jesus came into the world and showed by His teachings, miracles, and authority that He truly was the long awaited and prophesied Anointed One. And yet, at that time, as has been true ever since even up to the present day, some who truly encounter Jesus turn away from Him. Recall the Gospel story of the rich young man who approached Jesus asking how he might achieve eternal life.

> "Jesus said to him, 'Go, sell what you have and give to the poor, and you will have treasure in heaven. Then come, follow me.' When the young man heard this statement, he went away sad, for he had many possessions" (Matthew 19:16-22).

So for the sincere and dedicated believer, his faith in who Jesus was, and is, and always will be is truly a possession even more precious than his own mortal life. In the context of the Christian faith, life in this world is only the preparation work for eternal life.

Important Questions

Each newborn human being can be thought of as an artist's blank canvas. The choices one makes, the conscious thoughts one has, the places he goes, the things he does, and the things that happen to him, are the "brush strokes" that create the masterpiece of his life. Most people will eventually encounter, directly or indirectly, sooner or later, three basic questions about their existence: Where did I come from? Why am I here? Where am I going? Everyone realizes at some point, that life in this world is not permanent. It has for each one a specific beginning and an eventual end. So, where did I come from (is there a creator)? Why am I here (is there really any reason)? Where am I going (if anywhere)? And along with these questions one might encounter the profound query formally posed by the theologian and philosopher St. Thomas Aquinas, "Why does *anything* exist?"

I myself have "bumped into" these questions often enough in my own life to realize that they have, at least in part, led to the firm belief in God as my "be all and end all." Where did I come from? I'm convinced that I came from the plans and the will of the infinite and eternal mystery who is God, the Creator of all that ever was, and is, and ever will be. Why am I here? I'm convinced that I am here on this earth and in this life to search for and discover the reality of this mystery that allows all to exist – Almighty God Himself. Innumerable clues to His reality are present in the world around us. With that awareness, I feel committed to serving this One in ways that He directs me. And, where am I going? My conviction, faith, and confidence in the existence and almighty nature of God, leave me no doubt that I am going into eternity. It will be a state of existence that cannot be defined in the here and now. It cannot even be clearly imagined, but undoubtedly exists. My faith in the reality of God, and my hope in the goodness of His plans, allow me to live each moment and each day in this life with a joyous confidence that I will somehow be included in the infinite and eternal existence that is the joy and security of His presence.

And as for that ultimate question posed by St. Thomas, "Why does anything exist?", I can only stand in awe of an Almighty God who is such an unfathomable and incomprehensible mystery. Despite all of mankind's tremendous scientific efforts to find Him and know Him within the natural world in which we live, and in the context of time and space, God cannot and will not ever be fully known. But fortunately the human mind and heart can have an awareness that He does exist. He must exist based on all that we do know and observe and experience. Yes, we can become aware that there is a supernatural world existing beyond our natural world, and that the loving presence of God exists in both. All that mankind has ever discovered, or will ever discover, from the tiniest microscopic and chemical phenomena, to the facts pertaining to the deepest reaches of the cosmos, thousands of light years away, will never fully clarify who or how or why God really is.

We can come to have a sense, and even become convinced, that the reality of time and space within which we live and experience all things, exists within the real but incomprehensible elements of eternity and infinity. Fortunately, by our real experience of Jesus Christ, the Son of God, true God and true man, who was brought into the realm of time and space, and who lived with mankind by the plans of Almighty God, we are allowed to have immense hope that our God, the God of the Universe, will eventually include us in another realm – that of eternity and infinity. For me, the awesomeness of these concepts is so extreme, and so far removed from my common everyday thinking, that I can only reflect glancingly on them from time to time. Thank you, St.

Thomas, for opening this brilliant awareness of God's awesomeness to me!

For people who somehow come to different conclusions about the above questions, they may be left with the conviction that no such reality or direction exists (atheism), or that they can't really be sure if such a power exists (agnosticism). For those individuals, the end of life holds the specter of the end of existence in any sense. And for those who naively and innocently go through life not even considering the possibility of God existing, or the option of believing in Him, we can certainly hope and assume that there is also a Providential plan for them both now and in the hereafter.

For those who claim to have faith in God, they are convinced not only that He exists, but that He has something to say (ideally everything to say) in their lives, and in their afterlives. This is all the motivation they need to direct their lives now so that after their final breath, they will be judged as having been pleasing to the God of the Universe who created them to know, love, and serve Him in this life, so that they may eventually return to Him, and see Him "face-to-face," in the eternal Heavenly Kingdom. A sincere Godly faith can and does make one's life here in this world, right here and now, hopeful and joyful.

Holding On To The Faith

If one has been graced with the Christian faith, that confident certainty that God exists and was revealed by the life and works of Jesus Christ, how does he "hold on to" it? What needs to be done to maintain and even grow that faith? Like so many other matters in life – our physical fitness, our hygiene, our homes, our cars, our friendships, etc. – there are most certainly things that are required to maintain their goodness, integrity, and usefulness. So too it is with our faith.

In the area of physical fitness, only by a diligent program of repetitive and challenging exercise will one achieve and maintain a desired level of strength and stamina. Every car owner knows that the smooth workings and beautiful appearance of his vehicle requires regular attention to service intervals and detailing. So too our friendships require repeated renewals, especially in one's heart, but also by actual communication – a phone call; a lunch date; a family reunion or a class reunion; a Christmas card; a holiday, birthday, or anniversary gathering; an electronic message. We can probably all relate to having had a friend in grade school or high school that we had oh so seriously intended and hoped to keep in touch with "forever." For various reasons having to do with time, space, other commitments, and other directions in life, it just didn't happen. Our memories of that friend may still be fond, but if we were to unexpectedly encounter him today, we would feel so awkward in our conversation; so in a quandary as to what to talk about; so amazed as to how different that person seemed to have become. All of this because of the lack of contact and communication over the course of time.

In the area of faith, our "friendship" with God, we have so many opportunities to nourish it, to maintain it, and even to grow it. As Catholic Christians, we have a parent to guide us – we call her Holy Mother the Church. Based on the Christian Scriptures, the traditions of the Church as they have developed over the course of time, and the teaching authority of the Church as guided by our Holy Father the Pope and the urgings of the Holy Spirit, we can keep close to Jesus and His intentions for us. Holy Mother the Church provides us with specific Precepts (rules of conduct) that include: attend Mass on Sundays and Holy Days of Obligation; confess our sins; receive the Eucharist; observe fasting and abstinence; contribute to the material needs of the Church. She has set down these regulations not to make our lives in this world difficult, but rather for loving reasons – to make our lives disciplined so as to be able to focus on God, and the Godly things that we are meant to be doing.

We have the Mass which, to be sure, is the most important and most powerful prayer of the Catholic Church. We, His people, gather together, in part, for the purpose of proclaiming His greatness, praising Him, and asking for His mercy. But much more than this! We should be awestruck to realize what is actually happening at Mass. Through the Words of God that we hear in the Old and New Testaments, and especially, through the consecrated bread and wine that become the real Body and the real Blood of Jesus Christ, for us to consume and to be nourished by, amazing things are happening. We, the puny mortals that we are, become privileged to experience within our limited realm of time and space, the real and Almighty God of the Universe, in His realm of infinity and eternity. In the Mass, mortality and immortality meet. We can smile with joy, and feel the warmth and love of our God in all of His incomprehensible Being. And we can become certain of His caring and compassionate love and feel it flowing over us and into us. Said much more simply, in the Mass we "reach up" to the immortal and awesome God of the Universe, and He "reaches down" to us, the mortal and limited children that He created and loves so much, and with whom He wishes to be reunited in eternity. *Truly*, Heaven on Earth! Totally unique and wonderful! Don't miss it!

For the Mass-goer who not only attends Mass, but who listens attentively to the Biblical readings and the priest's homily, and *participates* in the prayers, and responses, and hymns, and the Eucharist, he cannot help but be both overjoyed and humbled by this experience. Again, *don't miss it!*

The word "Mass" is actually derived from the Latin word "missa" meaning "to send." We gather together to be educated, nourished, and inspired, *so that* we can be sent out into the world, to share the love of God with others and to live our lives in holiness as we anticipate eternity, eventually, with God in Heaven. And so, our priest concludes Mass by saying, "The Mass is ended. Go in peace to love and to serve the Lord." Said another way, our family gathering to be with our brother Jesus Christ and His Father and the Holy Spirit is completed. We have been nourished and inspired. Now go out into the world of God's people and share the Good News with all that you meet.

We also have the seven Sacraments to sustain and expand our faith. During His earthly sojourn, Jesus established these instruments of holiness to make real the powers of God within our limited realm of space and time. Through the Sacraments, the Life and Spirit of Jesus Christ, the Son of God, can remain with us always and everywhere. Although He ascended to His Father in Heaven, through the Sacraments and the action of God's love, the Holy Spirit, He remains with us here and now. Each Sacrament makes real what it symbolizes.

In the washing ceremony of Baptism the beginning Christian's soul is, in reality, cleansed of all sin, and that individual is provided with the opportunity to claim Jesus as Lord of his life. This claim requires total immersion into the ways and purposes of Jesus. In the Sacrament of Reconciliation the absolution given by the authority of the priest, who stands in the place of Christ, allows those sins that we commit due to our fallible human nature to be, in reality, forgiven by Almighty God. This leaves us spiritually cleansed and ready to undertake once again the sincere pursuit of our Lord's purposes. The symbols of bread and wine that are used in the Sacrament of Eucharist bring the real, glorified, and mystical Body and Blood of Jesus Christ from His infinite and eternal Heavenly existence, into the realm of our space and time, and into our mortal bodies. His presence within us strengthens us to know Him better, and to do His work in our lives. In Confirmation the symbol of being anointed with holy oil, in reality, infuses our souls with the Person of the Holy Spirit. We can thus become powerful with the love of God so that we can live and share the Good News of Jesus Christ. In the Sacrament of Holy Orders ordinary men who have discerned that they have a special call from God are ordained to the priesthood and, in reality, commit themselves to lifelong service to mankind as representatives of Jesus Christ in our midst. The vows spoken by a man and a woman in the Sacrament of Matrimony are for the purpose of binding them in a real and lifelong covenant of love for each other and a mutual consent to participate in family life by accepting children from God, educating them, and directing them in the ways of our faith. The Sacrament of the Sick blesses and anoints those who are in times of illness and poor health securing for them, in reality, a safe passage back to good health, or on to eternal life.

The Christian person who truly wants to hold on to his faith should also strive to become stronger in his personal spiritual habits. Inspirational Catholic author Matthew Kelly has written a book entitled *The Four Signs of a Dynamic Catholic*. In it, he puts forth several ways one can assure that his faith will be sincere and vibrant. First of all, he says, maintain a planned prayer life – every day dedicating a certain time, place, and method to communicate with the Lord. Secondly, one should be dedicated to learning about his faith and the Church by reading the writings of educated and authoritative Catholic authors. Thirdly, one needs to be committed to living a generous and authentic Christ-like life. One needs to make God and His purposes, as revealed by Jesus during His earthly life, the center, the pinnacle, and the sole purpose of his mortal existence. And finally, the dynamic Catholic will be the one who is so deep in His faith that he will tell others about it. He will evangelize. He will obey Jesus' command to "Go and make disciples of all nations" (Matthew 28: 18).

Center of My Life

Refrain: O Lord, you are the center of my life;
I will always praise you,
I will always serve you,
I will always keep you in my sight.

Keep me safe, O God, I take refuge in you,
I say to the Lord, "You are my God.
My happiness lies in you alone;
My happiness lies in you alone." *Refrain*

I will bless the Lord who gives me counsel,
Who even at night directs my heart.
I keep the Lord ever in my sight;
Since He is at my right hand,
I shall stand firm. *Refrain*

And so my heart rejoices, my soul is glad;
Even in safety shall my body rest.
For you will not leave my soul among the dead,
Nor let your beloved know decay. *Refrain*

You will show me the path of life,
The fullness of joy in your presence,
At your right hand, at your right hand
Happiness forever. *Refrain*

Chapter II:

"Be Not Afraid"

Courage

The root word for "courage" is "cor." The dictionary informs us that the old English and French languages used the word "corage" to refer to attributes of the heart and spirit. Further, it defines "courage" as: the attitude of facing and dealing with anything recognized as dangerous, difficult, or painful, instead of withdrawing from it; quality of being fearless or brave; valor. Courage has never been one of my strong suits – at least not in real life situations. In my imaginations and thoughts, I can be as courageous as the most courageous individuals. But when it comes down to planning active participation in "dangerous, difficult, or painful" events in life, I'm truly a chicken – fearful, anxious, and pulling away. I've always been this way. It's part of my personality; it's just who I am. I often attribute it to my basic introverted nature. As a child, there were mechanisms for avoiding such challenges. Just say, "No" (usually with many, many repetitions). Screaming, crying, or running away usually worked pretty well too. As an adolescent, saying "No," with an added excuse often worked well to get me out of difficult or overly challenging situations. But it was about this time, early in high school, that my love of God and friendship with Jesus brought me up against the command which I had heard repeatedly throughout my Catholic Christian experience, "Love God with your whole heart, your whole mind, and your whole soul," *and* "Love your neighbor as yourself" (Matthew 22:37).

In my own opinion at that time, I thought I was doing a reasonably good job on the first part, but I knew I was terribly lacking on the second part. Love of God seemed comfortable and natural. It was all mind and heart and soul work; you might call it "inside" work. Love of neighbor was certainly some of that, but much more required my time and effort; you might call it "outside" work. My introverted nature at that time resisted this "outside" work strongly. Nevertheless, because of the urgings of my friend Jesus, I managed to accept the challenge of being courageous and serving my neighbors with concern, generosity, and empathy by associating myself with the people and organizations that did so. In high school, there was the Legion of Mary. In college, the St. Vincent de Paul Society. In medical school, of course, I associated with the doctors and nurses who taught me the ways of serving the sick and suffering. Throughout these times, I often prayed that God would use these repeated and daily challenges of encountering my neighbor to suppress and even eradicate my self-centeredness, and make me outgoing, generous, and courageous. To some extent, this transformation has come about in my life, but I still have the need to take up my cross each and every day and to ask Jesus again to give me the courage in each and every situation, to be willing to encounter my neighbor and share God's goodness with him.

THY WILL BE DONE

Christ's Directive

The inspired authors of the four Gospels in the Christian scriptures, Matthew, Mark, Luke, and John, indicate the use of the directive, "Be not afraid," on over twenty occasions. It is most often
spoken by Jesus Himself, but at times it is also spoken by the an-
gels who announce certain of the events in Jesus' life. With such
frequency of repetition, we should come to be convinced that
God our Father seriously meant and still means for us to be
courageous in embracing and living out our faith in Him.

"Be not afraid" is a directive that has been read and considered
by Christians of all ages. In addition to the Gospels, this command
is heard in the other books of the New Testament and certainly in
the Old Testament as well. In modern times, our Sainted Pope,
John Paul II, chose these words as the theme and focus of his entire
twenty seven year pontificate – "Be not afraid." In his inaugural
homily, John Paul spoke to this theme saying, "Brothers and Sisters, do not be afraid to welcome Christ and accept His power.
Help the Pope and all those who wish to serve Christ, and with
Christ's power to serve the human person and the whole of
mankind. Do not be afraid. Open wide the doors for Christ. ... Do
not be afraid. Christ knows 'what is in a man.' He alone knows it."

Let's listen to some of the Gospel stories that include this sa-
cred directive.

•   •   •

Before the Incarnation, when God became man in the person of
Jesus of Nazareth,

"The angel Gabriel was sent from God to the virgin whose name was Mary. Coming to her, he said,

'Hail favored one! The Lord is with you.' But she was greatly troubled, then the angel said to her, '*Do not be afraid*, Mary, for you have found favor with God. Behold you will conceive in your womb and bear a son, and you shall name him Jesus. The Holy Spirit will come upon you, and the power of the Most High will overshadow you; for nothing will be impossible with God'" (Luke 1: 26-37).

When the pregnancy of Mary became apparent – a very socially and religiously unacceptable event in view of her unmarried status – an angelic message occurred again.

"When [Jesus'] mother Mary was betrothed to Joseph, but before they lived together, she was found with child through the Holy Spirit. Joseph, her husband, since he was a righteous man, yet unwilling to expose her shame, decided to divorce her quietly. Such was his intention when, behold, the angel of the Lord appeared to him in a dream and said, 'Joseph, son of David, *do not be afraid* to take Mary as your wife into your home. For it is through the Holy Spirit that this child has been conceived in her.' … When Joseph awoke, he did as the angel of the Lord had commanded him and took his wife into his home" (Matthew 1:18-24).

Once Jesus had been born, it was again an angel who made it known to mankind in the persons of the shepherds in the fields.

"The angel of the Lord appeared to them and the glory of the Lord shone around them, and they were struck with great fear. The angel said to them, '*Do not be afraid*; for behold I proclaim to you good news of great joy that will be for all the people. For today in the city of David a savior has been born for you who is Messiah and Lord'" (Luke 2:10-11).

As Jesus began His ministry, the Gospels reveal several scenarios in which He drew the Apostles to Himself as the cohort of twelve who eventually, by merit of this unique relationship, would initiate Christianity – the religion of imitating Jesus and following His teachings and His ways. But at the moment that each of the Apostles received his invitation to accept this unknown man as the long awaited Messiah, and leave behind his respective way of life, it must have been very anxiety provoking and fearful. In one such depiction, the weary and unsuccessful fishermen agreed to follow Jesus' request, and it changed their lives, as well as their eternities.

> "He said to Simon, 'Put out into the deep water and lower your nets for a catch.' Simon said in reply, 'Master, we have worked hard all night and have caught nothing, but at your command I will lower the nets.' When they had done this, they caught a great number of fish and their nets were tearing. ... When Simon Peter saw this, he fell at the knees of Jesus and said, 'Depart from me, Lord, for I am a sinful man.' ... Jesus said to Simon, '*Do not be afraid*; from now on you will be catching men.' ... They left everything and followed Him" (Luke 5:4-11).

The four Gospels tell us that Jesus was known to have performed many miracles. Those who received miracles, whether by their own requests or whether by the compassion of Jesus alone, expressed belief in Jesus as the Christ, the Holy One of God. The fear that they might have felt in the process of their conversion experience can be seen in the miracle that Jesus worked for a man named Jairus. This is written in the gospels of both Mark and Luke.

> "Someone from the synagogue official's house arrived and said, 'Your daughter is dead.' On hearing this, Jesus answered him, '*Do not be afraid*; just have faith and she will be saved.' When He arrived at the house he took her by the hand and called to her, 'Child, arise!' her breath returned and she immediately arose" (Luke 8:49-55; Mark 5:35-42).

Throughout the gospels, Jesus' confidence in God as a good and loving Father is always evident. His mission in this world included bringing this message to the Judaic people who often stood in fear of a powerful and controlling God. People of that mind set likely had strong feelings of uncertainty and fear in considering the possibility of letting go of the only faith that they and their ancestors had ever held. To accept Jesus' message of a caring, loving, and merciful God must have been extremely challenging. In one of His instructions, Jesus gave a strong reassurance of God's love for his people.

> "Therefore *do not be afraid* of them [the evil ones of the household]. Nothing is concealed that will not be revealed, nor secret that will not be known. What I say to you in the darkness speak in the light; what you hear whispered, proclaim on the housetops. And *do not be afraid* of those who kill the body but cannot kill the soul; rather be afraid of

the one who can destroy both soul and body in Gehenna. Are not two sparrows sold for a small coin? Yet not one of them falls to the ground without your Father's knowledge. Even all the hairs on your head are counted. So *do not be afraid*; you are worth more than many sparrows" (Matthew 10:26-31; Luke 12:3-7).

As Jesus encourages His listeners to let go of all the worldly things that they have been so accustomed to being attached to, and to pursuing in this world, He assures them that God as their Father really does care about them – very deeply, very truly, very individually, and very abundantly.

"Do not seek what you are to eat and what you are to drink, and do not worry anymore. Instead, seek His kingdom, and these other things will be given you besides. *Do not be afraid* any longer, little flock, for your Father is pleased to give you the kingdom. Sell your belongings and give alms" (Luke 12:29-33).

The Apostles were the twelve specially chosen by Jesus to be His closest friends in this world, and the protégés who would eventually carry on His message of Messiahship and Salvation to the whole world. So, we might imagine that in the course of the relatively short period of time that they spent with Him on the face of this earth (three years or so), questions about His true authority and power may have arisen. Jesus, being who He was, would have known this and would have realized the benefit of reassuring them in His actions and His words. Maybe this was His reason for approaching them on the stormy waters.

" … when they saw Him walking on the sea, they thought it was a ghost and cried out. They had all seen Him and were terrified. But at once He spoke with them, 'Take courage, it is I, *do not be afraid.*' He got into the boat with them and the wind died down" (Mark 6:50-51; John 6:19-20).

Peter, James, and John on the occasion of the Transfiguration account, could not possibly have known or even imagined when they went up the mountain with Jesus that day, that they would experience a powerful moment in all of Salvation history, whereby there would be a transition of God's people from the Old Covenant to the New Covenant. Moses and Elijah, representing the laws and the prophesies of ancient times, "conversed" with Jesus and then disappeared, leaving Jesus as the Only One – the One who came not to destroy but to fulfill the Old Covenant (Matthew 5:17). But the story clearly shows us that the three Apostles were troubled, anxious, and fearful.

"Then from the cloud came a voice that said, 'This is My beloved Son in whom I am well pleased; listen to Him.' When the disciples heard this, they fell prostrate and were very much afraid. But Jesus came and touched them, saying, 'Rise, and *do not be afraid.*' And when the disciples raised their eyes, they saw no one else but Jesus alone" (Matthew 17:5-8).

We can be sure of the tremendous relief and reassurance the three men felt that this unexpected and unimaginable event was over; and even more relieved that they had found themselves back in touch with the man and the friend that they knew they could trust. Their reflections on this event likely convinced them securely and once and for all that Jesus truly was both their friend and their Messiah, and the Messiah for all mankind and for all generations. Truly, the Son of God.

After experiencing the horrifying reality of Jesus death on the Cross, His apostles, disciples, family members, and friends were left with a terrible sense of emptiness. This event was the apparent loss of the One they were becoming so confident in to bring about such wonderful things as He had taught and demonstrated. But now He was gone. He was dead, and buried in a tomb with a huge bolder in front of it to seal it forever – or so it seemed. But the Gospels tell us of two women who wouldn't let it go; who wouldn't be so willing to accept this apparent terminal event.

> "After the Sabbath, as the first day of the week was dawning, Mary Magdalene and the other Mary (the mother of Joses) came to the tomb. And behold there was a great earthquake; an angel of the Lord descended from heaven, approached, rolled back the stone, and sat upon it. The guards were shaken with fear of him and became like dead men. Then the angel said to them, '*Do not be afraid.*' I know that you are seeking Jesus the crucified. He is not here, for He has been raised just as He said. Come and see the place where He lay. Then go quickly and tell His disciples, 'He has been raised from the dead, and He is going before you to Galilee; there you will see Him.' Then they went away quickly from the tomb, fearful yet overjoyed and ran to announce this to the disciples. And behold Jesus met them on their way and greeted

them. They approached, embraced His feet, and did Him homage. Then Jesus said to them, '*Do not be afraid.* Go tell my brothers to go to Galilee and there they will see me'" (Matthew 28:1-10).

Jesus knew that he would eventually separate from His disciples and His earthly confines and ascend to His Father in Heaven. He knew that this would generate fear and doubts in them. So, he prepared them for this by instructing them that He would be sending "another Advocate to be with you always, the Spirit of truth" (John 14:16-17). The Holy Spirit would accompany, bolster, and enliven them as they would go forth in the world to live in the faith of Jesus Christ, and share His purpose with others.

> "Peace I leave with you; my peace I give to you. Not as the world gives do I give it to you. *Do not let your hearts be troubled or afraid*" (John 14:27).

· · ·

For us to be committed Christians, we need to take courage in our faith and to become more like our Lord. Human nature tends instinctively to fear opposition, adversity, and threats. We often tend to react to such challenges in ways that avoid, escape from, or eradicate them. But in the realm of our spiritual identification, Jesus our Lord and Master, through the example of His life and the words of the Gospel testimonies, has instructed us to be fearless for His sake, and to be fearless in witnessing to Him as the Christ and the Holy One of God. By such behavior, true disciples of Christ will be encouraging others to recognize and come to accept Jesus the Christ as the Lord of their lives also.

Telling Others

In my own Christian walk, I have found that the most challenging and possibly the most fear-instilling call of my faith has been the discovery that I have, as does each and every baptized Christian person, a responsibility and a requirement to evangelize. I once thought that sharing the Good News of the Gospels was a call intended for only certain, "special" Christians. At the end of His ministry in this world, Jesus spoke to His Apostles leaving no doubt in their minds what it was that He expected of them after His Ascension to His Father.

> "All power in heaven and on earth has been given to me. Go, therefore, and make disciples of all nations, baptizing them in the name of the Father and of the Son, and of the holy Spirit, teaching them to observe all that I have commanded you. And behold I am with you always, until the end of the age" (Matthew 28:18-20).

What Jesus commanded of His disciples in that era, He commands of His disciples of all times. That includes you and me. If people who share our space and time in this world don't hear the Good News of Jesus' salvation work from us by our words and actions, they may never hear it at all, and they may never achieve eternal salvation.

> "Go into the whole world and proclaim the Gospel to every creature" (Mark 16:15).

I encourage each and every baptized Christian who reads these words to consider whether or not he truly claims and embraces his Baptism and the serious requirements it places on him. Do you realize the expectation that Baptism places on you to center your life on the purposes of Jesus Christ? To be immersed in the work of salvation has always been the intention of the Sacrament of Baptism. Each one needs to go out into the world, whatever is the sphere of his existence and influence, and speak with words and live by example, the message that is the Gospels – the Good News of Jesus Christ. God, as our Father, as His Son and our Lord, and as the Holy Spirit, loves us and is always with us. He has promised us the possibility of hope and contentment in this life, with salvation and joy in the eternal life.

For those who are not baptized, or who have been baptized but have not yet claimed and embraced their Baptism and have not yet made their faith the center of their lives, consider whether you are being called to do so. Will you, like His Apostles, "drop your nets" and follow Him by becoming "fishers of men"? Will you realize that the Jesus of history is the real person of God who can transform your life into a time of peace, and your eternity into happiness in God's never ending presence?

I hope each reader will take the time to study this book's "Appendix" to experience more about the Baptism-claiming process.

Be Not Afraid

You shall cross the barren desert,
but you shall not die of thirst.
You shall wander far in safety
though you do not know the way.
You shall speak your words in foreign lands
and all will understand.
You shall see the face of God and live.
Refrain: Be not afraid. I go before you always.
            Come, follow me, and I will give you rest.

If you pass through raging waters in the sea,
you shall not drown.
If you walk amid the burning flames
you shall not be harmed.
If you stand before the power of hell
and death is at your side,
know that I am with you through it all. *Refrain*

Blessed are your poor, for the kingdom shall be theirs.
Blest are you that weep and mourn, for one day
you shall laugh.
And if wicked tongues insult and hate you
all because of me, blessed, blessed are you! *Refrain*

Chapter III:

Serve Well!

What is Service?

Service includes all of the activities and efforts that provide for the needs and wants of others. If we look closely, we will find service going on in most areas of our daily lives: the cashier at the store, the waiter at the restaurant, the secretary at the office, the bus driver, the mailman, the school crossing guard, the dental hygienist, the auto mechanic, the airline stewardess, the nurse at the bedside. Just look and you'll find wherever you go, there are people performing service, providing for the needs and wants of others.

Many careers that people choose for their way of life, are service oriented: teachers, lawyers, doctors, nurses, pilots, clergy, therapists, etc., etc. Some who pursue such careers are motivated by humanitarian concerns. Others do so for financial return, or social status, or personal gains.

Performing such service tasks obviously does not require one to be a Christian. Many who serve, do so for other than Christ-motivated reasons. Perhaps it's a way to obtain the paycheck that sustains their life. Perhaps it's a gratifying "feel-good" way to use the knowledge and skills they've worked to acquire. Perhaps it's a means to an end, climbing the ladder of worldly success. Whatever one's motivation for performing the service, it doesn't detract from or change the reality that other people are being helped in some way. But the focus that I mean to establish by entitling this third principle, "Serve Well!", is to serve as our Lord Himself would serve and as He would want us to serve His people – willingly, patiently, generously, joyously. For the true Christian, to serve others should be something that he wants to do to please his God, who commands us to love Him and to love our neighbors. For the true Christian, to serve others should not be just for what he can get out of it – a paycheck, a promotion, a compliment, or a sense of accomplishment. In it's best form, service should be done with a sincere concern for the welfare of the other. It should be done with the desire to imitate Jesus Christ, our Lord and Savior, and for the greater glory of God our Creator and Almighty Father.

First Experiences

In my own life, I have at one time or another been employed, and worked in jobs where I carried out tasks prescribed by my employer. If I performed that work as specified, I would get a paycheck every two weeks. Although I recall having enough character to always do a good job – as complete and as thorough as I possibly could – I was never aware that any certain attitude was necessary in order to get my paycheck. I do recall wanting to please my employer simply because he had been willing enough just to hire me and to pay me, and I didn't want to disappoint him. Now looking back on those times, I realize very clearly that I was performing service, not only for my employer by helping him attain the business goals he had in mind, but I was also serving the people whom his business served. Providing care for animals at the boarding kennel, was serving those who left their pets in the hands of the veterinarian. Laboring for the pool contractor, was serving those who would eventually enjoy swimming in those pools. Working in the meat factory and delivering their products, was serving those who would eventually consume and be nourished by those products. As an orderly at the hospital, I was not only serving the patients to whom I was assigned, but also serving the nurses whose duties I was helping to carry out.

I knew at the times that I worked these jobs that I really enjoyed having designated responsibilities and carrying them out. I also knew that I enjoyed receiving a paycheck and the feeling of accomplishment that it gave me. I know in my years since those times, I have been consciously focused on being open to the will of God and serving Him and His people in whatever ways He has planned for me, and with the attitude that Jesus Himself would have.

What Some Others Say

One of the most unselfish servants in our modern world has been Blessed Mother Teresa. She provided care – physical, emotional, and spiritual care – for the poor, the sick, and the dying in the streets of Calcutta, India. She has often been quoted as having encouraged would-be servants to consider, "Everyone we serve is Jesus in disguise."

• • •

Inspirational Catholic speaker, Father Larry Richards, speaking on a compact disc presentation entitled "Knowing God's Will," addresses the concern of how to know and live God's will. He states that what God wants of us, always has to do with love and with service. If the action or decision being considered is not for the love of God and neighbor, or not for the service of God and neighbor, then it is not of God. It is Father Larry's understanding and conviction that God's will for each and every one of us, His children, is to be holy. Our Church identifies this concept as "the universal call to holiness." We are to identify God as our source and as our destiny, and we are to make Him the center and prime purpose of our lives. We are to become more and more like Him as we live out our limited worldly lives, being fully aware of our eventual transition into our infinite and eternal lives. The old time Baltimore Catechism puts it this way: "Who made us? God made us." "Why did God make us? God made us to know, love and serve Him in this world, and to be happy with Him in the next."

Father Richards says that it is God's will for each of us to be holy and to go to Heaven. Each one is called to be a person of love and of service. If we are not serving, we are not in the will of God. To be holy is to will what God wills. His will and my will must become one. Such a conviction and plan for this life will lead us to eternal life in Heaven. It will lead us to sainthood.

• • •

In modern times, spiritual master, author, and professor Henri Nouwen, inspires us about the life of service in his book *Show Me the Way*, when he writes, "The great mystery of God's compassion is that in His entering with us into the condition of a slave, He reveals Himself to us as God. In the emptied and humbled Christ we encounter God, we see who God really is, we come to know His true divinity. Servanthood is God's self-revelation. Radical servanthood is not an enterprise in which we try to surround ourselves with as much misery as possible, but a joyful way of life in which our eyes are opened to the vision of the true God who chose the way of servanthood to make Himself known." Further he writes, "Joy and gratitude are the qualities of heart by which we recognize those who are committed to a life of service in the path of Jesus Christ. Wherever we see real service we also see joy, because in the midst of service a Divine Presence becomes visible and a gift is offered." And then he points out, "in prayer we meet Christ, and in Him all human suffering. In service we meet people, and in them the suffering Christ."

The Servant Savior

It is not difficult to see, when we read the four Gospels, that Jesus' life and mission was focused on service to God His Father, and on service to all of mankind. The love He had for God His Father and for all mankind is what motivated His life of service. The Gospel writers emphasize the high priority that Jesus had on service in His actions and as His way of life when we hear the Lord say,

> "Anyone who wants to become great among you must be your servant and anyone who wants to be first among you must be your slave, just as the Son of man came not to be served but to serve, and to give his life as a ransom for many" (Matthew 20:26-28; Mark 10:45).

> Matthew 23:11-12 emphasizes and reiterates, "The greatest among you must be your servant. Anyone who raises himself up will be humbled and anyone who humbles himself will be raised up."

One of the very best and well known examples of the type of service that Jesus expects of us as His disciples is revealed by the Gospel writer Luke in the parable of the Good Samaritan. We are told that this story was presented by Jesus in response to the scholar who questioned our Lord as to who was to be considered as his neighbor, so that he might serve him, as the Law commanded. Jesus responded with the description of a man who fell victim to robbers as he was on his way down the road from Jerusalem to Jericho.

> "They stripped and beat him and went off leaving him half-dead. A priest happened to be going down that road, but when he saw him, he passed by on the opposite side. Likewise a Levite came to the place, and when he saw him, he passed by on the opposite side. But a Samaritan traveler who came upon him was moved with compassion at the sight. He approached the victim, poured oil and wine over his wounds and bandaged them. Then he lifted him up on his own animal, took him to an inn and cared for him. … Which of these three, in your opinion, was neighbor to the robbers' victim? He answered, 'The one who treated him with mercy.' Jesus said to him, 'Go and do likewise'" (Luke 10:29-37).

In the Gospel of John (13:12-17), we can read about one particular work of humble service which Jesus performed for His Apostles. On the night before He would give Himself up to worldly authorities, and then die to redeem all of mankind, Jesus shared supper with His Apostles. When the meal was done, Jesus arose from the table and began to wash their feet. The washing of feet, we are told by Rev. James Martin, S.J., in his book *Jesus: A Pilgrimage*, at the time "was seen as a mark of hospitality, but also a menial task often performed by slaves to welcome a dignitary hosted by the slave's master. To the disciples it would have been an unmistakable demonstration of humility, something an inferior would do for a superior." After Jesus washed the disciples' feet, we are told, He reclined at table again, and said to them, "Do you know what I have done to you? You call me Teacher and Lord – and you are right, for that is what I am. So if I, your Lord and Teacher, have washed your feet, you also ought to wash one another's feet. For I have set you an example, that you also should do as I have done to you. Very truly, I tell you, servants are not greater than their master, nor are messengers greater than the one who sent them. If you know these things, you are blessed if you do them."

In discussing this act of Jesus' service, Father Martin asks his readers to re-read the last line of this passage, "If you know these things, you are blessed if you do them." Father Martin points out that, "Jesus asks them to move from knowledge to action. It takes the form of a command; Jesus is speaking as Teacher and Lord, from a position of authority. So the disciples are expected to heed his message: It's not enough to have knowledge of Christ, you must let it inform your life's decisions. Blessedness comes not only from words and thoughts, but also from deeds. Or as St. Ignatius Loyola wrote, 'Love shows itself more in actions than in words.'"

Literally everything we hear Jesus say, and see Him do in the Gospel verses, can be appreciated as being service to God His Father and to mankind, His brethren. Whether he was teaching, working miracles, praying, suffering, dying, rising from the dead, or ascending into Heaven, everything he did was service to the Father and to mankind. And Jesus did so to reveal to mankind the love and mercy of God. All of the New Testament is truly a testament to the holy service of Jesus Christ – dedicated, focused, and unfailing, holy service. His was the life from which we can learn to "Serve well!"

Make Me a Channel of Your Peace

Make me a channel of your peace.
Where there is hatred, let me bring your love.
Where there is injury, your pardon, Lord,
and where there's doubt, true faith in you.

Make me a channel of your peace.
Where there's despair in life, let me bring hope.
Where there is darkness, only light,
and where there's sadness, ever joy.

Oh, Master, grant that I may never seek
so much to be consoled as to console.
To be understood as to understand.
To be loved as to love with all my soul.

Make me a channel of your peace.
It is in pardoning that we are pardoned,
in giving of ourselves that we receive,
and in dying that we're born to eternal life.

CONCLUSION

As an older married couple, Patty and I have long since finished raising our children. But I'd like to think that we are still influencing them in good and Godly ways. Each of them has encountered so many spiritual and secular situations. Each of them has made relationship commitments, career choices, and faith decisions. Each of them is, as we say, "traveling down the road of life." It is my deepest and most sincere prayer and hope that each of them will eventually find eternal salvation in the Holy and Heavenly Kingdom that God, the Father, the Son, and the Holy Spirit, has intended for them, and for all of us, since before the beginning of time.

I'm thoroughly convinced that Christians who treasure and nurture their spirituality will indeed be able to "Hold on to (their) faith." Those who maintain a courageous attitude about, and confidence in, the will of God can certainly expect to live their lives "Be(ing) Not Afraid." And those who have truly encountered Jesus Christ, will imitate Him and "Serve Well!" They will transmit the goodness of God to their neighbors. I believe that those who are diligent in living these three principles will be coming to "know, love, and serve God in this world," and will be preparing "to be happy with Him in the next."

. . .

"Peace be with you. Jesus said to them again, "Peace be with you. As the Father has sent me, so I send you. Receive the holy Spirit" (John 20:19-22).

Appendix:

Claim Your Baptism

In several portions of the preceding chapters, the reader has heard about the concept of claiming and embracing his Baptism. Presently, I wish to clarify and impress on you even more clearly what this really means.

With very little reflection, each baptized Christian can certainly assure himself that there was indeed a specific point in time when his baptismal event occurred. Beyond that moment, many people, be they younger or older, will go on with their lives without much, if any, further thought about their Baptism. Maybe there's an assumption that now they are in the "club" of Christianity and all will be well. But truly, to be in the club and to be working with and for the club (as with any club), are considerably different states of mind and commitment.

To be a member of the Church is not meant to be a privileged position which in some way gives us magical assurance of eventual Heavenly reward. Rather, it is a grace, a gift from God. We have, each one of us, somehow been endowed with the Christian faith, and now, because of our Baptism, we have both the opportunity and the responsibility to imitate Christ. To live as Christ lived.

To do what Christ would do. To discover and to live out the law of love for God and neighbor.

The constant and unchangeable Christian law of love is meant to be consciously and always our focus. For one to say, "Because I was baptized, 'I've got it made' as far as eternal salvation," is not acceptable, and is not the way a fully informed and motivated Christian should be living. Rather, for one to say, "Because I was baptized, I've got a lifelong responsibility to imitate Jesus Christ, to show His love, and to spread His love in whatever way God has planned for me," that is the true and full meaning of being baptized.

It is not only the act of, at one point in time, having submitted to, or having been submitted to, a washing ceremony. As importantly, it is at one point in time, having accepted in the depths of one's heart the distinct focus on, and commitment to, living powerfully every moment of every day for the purposes of God, as He was revealed to us by the earthly life and works of His only Son, Jesus Christ. This, then, is what is meant by claiming one's Baptism.

To be baptized literally means to be immersed. When one decides to be part of the Christian way of life, as when one decides to be part of most anything he considers to be a high priority in his life, it is very important to be totally dedicated to it. And so, the idea of immersion is certainly appropriate. If we are surrounded on all sides – left and right, top and bottom, front and back – we have no other way to respond to whatever we encounter, other than by that which surrounds us. In Baptism, we are to be fully immersed in, and surrounded by, the life and purposes of Jesus Christ, thus being committed to responding to every person and situation as Jesus Himself would.

For many, being baptized as infants, there would have been no recollection of the event and there would have been no opportunity to understand at the time what it was about, much less to make a choice as to whether or not to be baptized for Jesus Christ. For some, an adult awareness and decision may have been made, but it may not have been made in a sincere and committed sense that would allow them to maintain a secure, lifelong connection. And perhaps for those whose original commitment was very sincere, the ongoing demands, stresses, and distractions of life in this world, may have caused them to loosen their connection, and thereby fall away from that commitment.

Whichever of these scenarios may have taken place, one who desires to be fully Christian must at some point claim his Baptism, meaning to consciously decide to immerse himself in the challenges and the ways of Jesus Christ as we know them from their only source – the New Testament.

An image that may help to convey this immersing nature of Baptism might be the idea of a swimming pool. To stand on the side of the pool and think about being in the water may be pleasant, but it is certainly nothing like once having made the decision to jump into the water, one actually does so, and becomes completely immersed in it. He thereby gains the full experience of being in the water. In making this act of will to jump into the water, the individual commits himself to responding to the water that surrounds him. He immediately begins to act in ways directed by the nature of water. He will now breathe and move his arms and legs in ways that are much different than when he was standing on the side of the pool. He will now be refreshed by the water, and he will survive in it.

The faithful Christian who makes the decision to "jump into" his baptismal event, and to claim his Baptism as his own sincere commitment, will gain the full experience of being in the life of Christ. He will quickly learn to respond to everything he thinks and does in the ways directed by the nature of Jesus Christ. And he will be refreshed spiritually here and now, and will survive in the afterlife when he is in the heavenly Kingdom which God has made available through the life and works of his Son.

Conversely, if one remains fearful of "jumping into" his Baptism and remains "standing on the side" of his Christian faith because it seems to be pleasant and sufficient, he will never fulfill the intentions of Jesus– that is, to be fully committed to Him, and fully immersed in His ways. The end results could be disastrous in his eternity.

•　•　•

Let me present a few considerations for anyone who wishes to have a better sense of whether or not he is willing to claim his Baptism. Think first about this concept of immersion. Am I willing to consider living a holy life modeled on the Gospels of Jesus Christ, and to consider that as my top priority always and everywhere? Do I truly wish to dedicate myself to the idea of making Christ-like living the center and focus of my entire life? It is certainly possible but it takes a serious and sincere lifelong personal commitment. During the course of His ministry, Jesus asked His Apostles, and He asks of all who wish to be His disciples, "Can you drink from the cup that I drink, or be baptized with the baptism with which I am baptized?" (Mark 10:38). Jesus was always immersed in the work of His Father. Can we commit to immersing ourselves always in the work of His Father, too? Like with Jesus, such a commitment, such an immersion, will lead to certain challenges, and difficulties in this life, but also like with Jesus, it will lead us to the eternal Heavenly reward which we all desire – eternal peace and happiness in the presence of God Himself.

Now let me ask a few questions to encourage you in reflecting on your own baptismal event. Pause for a moment after each question in order to make the recollection of your Baptism more meaningful.

When were you baptized?

How old were you?

Where was your Baptism performed?

Who performed it?

Who were your Godparents?

Who else was with you?

Were there photographs of you being baptized?

If you were an infant, realize that at that moment, your parents were claiming you for Christ. Are you now ready to claim yourself for Christ? Do you want your faith in God to be the center of who you are?

If you were of adult years when you were baptized, how did you feel about your Baptism then?

Have you reflected on your baptismal decision and your baptismal event since then? Has the reason for your getting baptized grown in importance for you since then?

Take a few moments now to think of yourself being in a Church where the Sacrament of Baptism might be taking place. Think of yourself approaching the baptismal font with slightly anxious but excited and convincing thoughts that you are about to immerse yourself in the life and purposes of Jesus Christ. Think of yourself now standing at the font, and now leaning over. Feel the water pour over your head. "In the name of the Father, and of the Son, and of the Holy Spirit." As you stand up, feel the water running into your eyes and down your face. Feel a distinct chill, realizing the power of the Holy Trinity – Father, Son, and Holy Spirit – has come upon you.

And now, renew the promises that you made, or were made for you, at the time of your actual Baptism. By responding affirmatively to these questions, you are promising to live the rest of your life immersed in Godliness through the ways of Jesus Christ. You will be claiming yourself for Jesus Christ, and you yourself will be claiming your Baptism.

"Through the Pascal Mystery we have been buried with Christ in Baptism, that we may walk with Him in the newness of life. And so, let us renew the promises of Holy Baptism, by which we once renounced Satan and his works and promised to serve God in the holy Catholic Church. And so I ask you:

Do you renounce Satan?

And all his works?

And all his empty show?

Do you believe in God, the Father Almighty, Creator of heaven and earth?

Do you believe in Jesus Christ, His only Son, our Lord, who was born of the Virgin Mary, suffered death, and was buried, rose again from the dead and is seated at the right hand of the Father?

Do you believe in the Holy Spirit, the holy Catholic Church, the communion of saints, the forgiveness of sins, the resurrection of the body and life everlasting?

May Almighty God, the Father of our Lord Jesus Christ, who has given us new birth by water and the Holy Spirit and bestowed on us forgiveness of our sins, keep us by His grace in Christ Jesus our Lord, for eternal life. Amen."

You now realize, and are fully convinced, that the rest of your life will have but one purpose – to live out the love and the will of God. With the certainty and power of your newly claimed Baptism, you are now sent out into the world "to love and to serve the Lord."

Bibliography

A Retreat for Lay People, Ronald A. Knox, Ignatius Press, 2011

Catechism of the Catholic Church, St. Paul Books and Media, 1994

Forming Intentional Disciples, Sherry A. Weddell, Our Sunday Visitor Publishing Division, 2012.

Jesus – A Pilgrimage, James Martin, S.J., Harper-Collins Publishers, 2014.

Jesus of the Gospels, Arthur E. Zannoni, St. Anthony Press, 1996

Knowing the Will of God, Fr. Larry Richards, The Reason For Our Hope Foundation, C.D.

Show Me the Way, Henry J.M. Nouwen, Crossroad Publishing Company, 1997

The Four Signs of a Dynamic Catholic, Matthew Kelly, Beacon Publishing, 2012

The New American Bible, Benziger Publishing Company, 1991

Webster's New World Dictionary, Second College Edition, Simon and Schuster